Je Te Remercie

Miranda Forster

Published by L.M. Forster, 2020.

JE TE REMERCIE

First edition. June 14, 2020.

ISBN: 978-1393897576

Written by Miranda Forster.

This is dedicated to my family, especially my mother who instilled in me the writing of poetry is cathartic, my children, who helped me to see the world in different ways, and my husband, who taught me I was worthy of love.

Foreword

GROWING UP IN RURAL Georgia may seem like a strange thing to inspire a young girl to write poetry, but that is what is true for me. My mother always enjoyed writing both prose and poetry, and I suppose I just took after her. Somewhere amongst her things at home she has stored away the first Haiku I ever wrote and a few other odds and ends of my early writings—stories I wrote because I finished all my school work early and was told to sit in the back of the room and write or draw, where I would not disturb and distract others.

So, I did. And I was lucky enough to have teachers who encouraged me to keep doing it. In eighth grade, I wrote my first letter to the editor—a piece inspired by an episode of Little House on the Prairie in which young Laura Ingalls attends the country fair on the Walnut Creek church grounds. The girls rolled hoops and had stitching contests; the women traded farm goods and won prizes for baking, while the men competed at chopping logs and barrel walking. The praise I received from my teacher for having that letter published, along with her encouragement, led me to my first career in newspaper journalism. Writing just seemed to be in my blood. And any time, throughout life, that a particularly strong emotion took over or vivid experience occurred, I turned to writing poetry. Muses presented themselves to me periodically, and when they did, I wrote. Early on, my poetic muse was often a boyfriend. As I grew, I wrote about many other things as well—music, children, nature, fairies.

I should also mention that in seventh grade, I fell in love with my first foreign language studied: French. I went on to study French for many more years, and also took three years of Latin and two years of college Spanish. (My husband is fluent in Spanish, and we have some interesting conversations in English, Spanish, and French all meshed together). My love of language leads me, from time to time, to write in another language, usually French, but occasionally Spanish. This is my collection, so far, of poems written from 1987 to the present. It's just me sharing my thoughts with you, from when I was a teenager, through my first marriage (and divorce), to having children, and taking a nearly nine-year emotional and sexual hiatus, to finding myself again, reawakening, and finding true love after all.

The Storm (1987)

The atmosphere
Reminds me of my mind
Swept into fury by one
Small phrase—"I love you."
How can something
That means so much
Mean so little to our
Inhumane nature—
Carried in greed
And destruction by carnal
Desires and lust.
Like the angry winds
And lightning of the storm
Destroys the earth—
The false meaning of the phrase destroys
People: their emotions
And their lives!

Imprint (1988)

I watched you yesterday,
When we were riding.
It is fitting that you
Always ride a stallion.
A graceful, determined animal;
Your personalities match.
Your movements clasp and flow together.
Your body holds a straight perfect line,
Never strained.
The stallion moves with ease;
A swift, agile gait
Typical of his breed.
The sight moved me
And I wanted to reach out
And test reality—but I didn't
For fear the scene would disappear.
It's imprinted on my mind,
Perfectly—the way you fit together—
You and the stallion.
I recall the sight now and then.
And I want to go to you—
To touch you and feel how the countryside
Fits inside you.
You even smell of the country,

Fresh and crisp, but dusty, rugged.
Like the smell of hay and horses and soap.
Yes—it is fitting that you
Always ride a stallion.
I felt it, as I watched you yesterday,
When we were riding.

Loneliness (1988)

Loneliness surrounds my being.
With each second passes a thousand years.
Apart from you, I am nothing.
Please save me from the
Endless void—loneliness.
Come love me. I need you.
Please, let me return your love.
With all my soul and heartfelt strength,
I love you.
I miss you. I am lonely.
When again I see you,
Love me with your all.
Heart, soul, body, and mind
Just as I love you.
Then, never leave again.

The Erl King (1988)

My fingers touch the keys,
And excitement begins.
My body is swayed by the emotion.
The height progresses
As the sound of hoofbeats fills my mind.
A man cries out in anguish.
Death is coming to steal his son away.
I feel the father's passions
As evil draws nearer.
The boy speaks—
The Erl King lulls and sings him to sleep.
The tones fall quickly to pianissimo.
The fight is over;
Death has won.
The piece ends,
And I begin to cry...

Only in Time (a sonnet assigned in English class 1989)

I WATCH THE CLOUDS drift by in sorrow deep.
    They used to seem so beautiful and calm.
    But now, they rain and drab grey color keep.
    My heart no longer senses quiet balm,
    For thou discerned that happy would you be
    By staying in my home and heart no more.
    Only in time has thou forgotten me.
    I watch you pass, who once I so adored,
    Knowing that somehow there must be a way
    To once again retain thy gracious love.
    Rushing, I go to ask if you would stay.
    My voice falls sweetly, softly as a dove.
    And then thy vows tell me that it should seem,
    Of forgetting me, that thou couldst only dream.

The Stallion (1989)

I COULD NOT PUT UP fences
    And keep you from the world.
    For you're a mighty stallion
    That needs the world to run.
    You stand so tall and proud;
    Head held high, tail extended;
    Racing with the wind.
    I hoped to hold you but a day.
    I found too late, my feelings
    Were for that too strong.
    I have reined the stallion
    Who was so proud and tall.
    I held the tether tightly.
    I could not set you free.
    Freedom to roam is all
    That you would ask of me.

Now I hold the reins, but
I never meant to bind you.
Yet I had never known
Such a wonderful beast.
And now you find
You are glad to be
Running free
Within my fences.
I, the happiest
One alive
See that now
The stallion loves me, too.

The Gardener (1990)

MY LOVE IS LIKE A GARDEN
    That grows with each new day.
    Your laughter is the shower
    That makes each blossom burst.
    Your eyes and glowing, loving face
    Are the sun that warms my love.
    Your gentle touch and tender smile
    Are the breezes blowing.
    Your subtle scent that only you have
    Is my flower's perfume.
    Only you can make the
    Love inside me grow.
    And you, indeed, have proved
    To be a succcssful gardener.

Rebirth (1988)

I DIED ONCE...A YEAR ago.
  It took a stranger
  To pull me out of my
  Self-made grave.
  He took my hand and
  Held it gently.
  As he prodded deep
  Into my soul.
  He bade me tell him
  All my fears,
  All my sorrows,
  And my pain.
  And as I unfolded
  My story to him
  He threw them all away.
  I learned from him
  How not to die:
  Don't bring it on myself.
  I tell you that I died once,
  Because I was living
  For someone else,
  Which isn't living at all.

Disheartened (2009)

WONDROUS WORLD, WEIGHT upon my shoulders
Why must I feel others' pain?
My heart feels no joy today.
I must plod on. I must plod on.
An end is an end is an end,
But this is simply the beginning.

Disillusionment (2003)

YOUR BETRAYAL MAKES me see you
> For who you really are.
> Rapacious, dispassionate.
> But not for everyone else.
> My world careens
> In the blitz of your cruelty.
> Find a catharsis!
> Move on—move on.

On Writing Poetry (2008)

BEHOLD! THE POWER OF words
    Encompassing you with emotions
    You didn't know you had.
    The windows to the soul,
    Not the eyes as belied
    All these years, but words,
    Which can be read by others
    Long after you are gone.

November Sadness (2008)

MOVING IN SILENT SOLITUDE, the depression wandered in the shadows
Stalking her prey like it was scoured—
She beat down upon the darkness,
Looked like a woman gone mad.
Emotions run amok, turned bitter,
As it seethed and grew.
What power holds the depression?
"Contemplate" screamed her conscience!
Not a horror ever was known as feeling perdulous as this
Searing hearts in its path like a dragon in dry grass.
She spun out of bliss, the head of a forgotten daisy trailing behind;
Sank down where tears and bitterness abide.
Emotions heaped in a quagmire—
Distinct but intangible,
Crucifying her for forgetting them one by one.
Hope is not a morning dove,
Rather a mourning prong
Standing ready to pierce the heart; cause pain.
Her Achilles tendon, becoming this Desdemona,
Reeling, reveling.
O! Melancholy world,
You have guillotined me again.

Pour Vous (2011)

Merci. Pour simplement être un ami
Quand j'ai eu besoin d'un.
Vous m'acceptez quand j'a pensé
Que ces jours ont été allés.
Vous me voyez pour moi.
Encore, je vous remercie.

Dance of the Fae (2006)

Where the forest meets the meadow
The faeries come to dance
Wild beautiful and delicate
Things unseen by human eye
Are gathered in the splendor of fall

Autumn Garden (2008)

Yearning
Is a wistful peacock
Gliding lightly, tail flowing behind
In the misty autumn morning
Crying, calling to his love.

Fairies (2003)

WHAT IF FAIRIES DANCED in your room?
　　I might steal a glance.
　　What if they crept into the garden under the moon?
　　I could find their footprints.
　　What if they played in leaf piles?
　　I would find fairy dust in your hair.
　　What if fairies danced in your room?

Autumn (2008)

PAINTED ON THE FORESTS with
    The first wisp of coolness
    It burnishes the world
    With its glorious colors
    Covering the earth
    Then withers away with
    The coming frosts.

Daughters (2009)

SISTERS
    Frolic freely
    Dress-up playmates for life
    Laughter, fulfillment fill the air
    Best friends

Fairies (2009)

I WONDER IF THEY LIKE being whispered about?
    I suppose they do.
    The always flee at the hint of human presence;
    They never let us see.
    Some people say they don't exist.
    They make me ponder the thought.

A Mother's Wisdom (2009)

MY MOTHER ONCE TOLD me
   "You'll have daughters of your own some day"
   And then I'd know
   What great sorrows come
   From such great joys.
   "Hmpf!" I said. "I'll never be like you."
   Why are mothers always right?
   I take back everything I've said.

A Fall Memory (2000)

I REMEMBER THE CAMPFIRE ring
    I remember finding it there in the woods
    I remember sifting through the ashes
    And finding the curled opossum's tail.
    I remember laughing with my mother, and
    I remember thinking, How gross!"
    I remember saying the hobo must have enjoyed his meal.
    Even as the first fall breezes blow
    I remember that walk, that encounter.

Toujours (2011)

JE VOUS AI TOUJOURS aimé.
> J'ai gardé mon coeur contre ces
> Sentiments toutes ces années.
> Mais un regard dans ces yeux parfaits,
> Et je ne peux pas les supprimer plus longtemps.
> Mon désir arden test retourné dans un marée.
> Seulement un mot, seulement une etreinte,
> Et moi seraient seulement a vous pour toujours.

Tentation (2011)

LA TENTATION ME TIENT au coeur.
    Comme j'ai envie de marcher encore à côté de toi,
    La main dans la main.
    Je me rappelle bien des bons
    Moments que nous avons eus,
    Les rires, le plaisir de sentir
    Ton cœur bat en même temps que le mien.
    Et te revoir pour la première fois,
    Les frissons me reviennent.

Tu (2011)

TON YEUX BLEUS
    Ton cheveux blond,
    Ton mains doux.
    Sont les choses que j'adore.
    Ton coeur fort,
    Ton courage puissant,
    Ton esprit genereux.
    Sont les choses qu j'aime.
    Ton etreinte forts,
    Ton embrasses chaud,
    Ton passion ardente.
    Sont les choses que je désir.

I am (2014)

I am forty-three.
I am strong and independent
But not strong enough
To understand your private pain.
Being young was so much harder than this.
I feel your plight
But can never get it.
Just don't shut me out.

You may be surprised
By the similarity of our
Teenage experiences.
You and I are not so
Different, after all.
We just lived in two
Different times.
Just don't shut me out.

How can I help you
Through it,
My beautiful daughter?
All my hopes and
Dreams are rolled up
Into the two of you.
I want to see you

Learn and grow
From this adversity.
Just don't shut me out.

Reawakening (2015)

I cannot comprehend
The power you hold
Over me, but I
Will relish in it;
Delight in the reawakening
Of my spirit.

Every thought of you
Is like the kindling
Of a small flame;
I am enraptured
By its glow.

New Emotion (2015)

There is a new emotion
Dwelling within—
This fondness I have
Come to cherish.
A friendship taking
New hold and
Sparking into a fresh
Flame; burning
More brightly than
I ever imagined
Or hoped to feel again.

Daydreams (2015)

All week, I have missed
The feel of my hand in yours.
Fingers interlaced;
Palm to palm.

Each night, I remember
Having slept in your arms.
Legs all tangled,
Synchronized breaths.

Each day, I think of you
And smile to myself.
Awake, yet dreaming—bliss.

This (2015)

THIS...WHATEVER IT is,
    Consumes my every waking thought.
    I am awed, still, that I even
    Went through with it—
    The lover's tryst that
    Sparked long-forgotten emotion
    Back to life and renewed
    My spirit; made me soar.
    Your incredible, sensitive soul,
    Unmasked and bared
    To me without a care,
    And I unveiled the
    Whole of me.
    Raw, sensual,
    Pure and powerful,
    There is an evolution
    Beginning there.

I Never (2016)

I NEVER IMAGINED—NOT for one second—
That I would fit so well in your arms.
I never dreamt I might
Feel such longing to be there.
I never hoped that I would find
Happiness in your embrace.
I never thought of simple
Conversations of seductions.
I never glimpsed passion
So real, so raw.
I never imagined; I never dreamt;
I never hope; I never thought;
I never glimpsed...
Until there was you.

Easy (2016)

LIFE WOULD BE SO EASY
    If being with you
    Had never begun
    To heal my broken heart.

To Be Yours (2016)

Having known you
Having touched you
Having felt you
I long to be yours.

I want to be in your arms.
I want to taste your lips.
I want to feel your breath.
I long to be yours.

I long to be yours...
To be yours.

Found Poem – On Falling in Love (2015)

WE'LL BE FINE AFTERWORD.
   Just like we were before.
   What makes you think so?
   I know we will.
   You don't have to be afraid.
   I've known lots of people
   Who have done it.
   And afterward, they were
   All so happy.
   (from Hemingway's Hills Like White Elephants)

Untitled (2015)

JE LANGUIS DE VOUZ-voir tous le jours.
    Mais ceci n'est pas possible encore.
    Je languis pour vous dire je t'aime
    Mais vous netes pas pret a l'entendre.
    Donc, je vais attendre
    Un jour, vouz languirez pour le meme.
    Et puis je marcherai dans mon avenir.

Don't (2015)

DON'T ASK ME NOT TO fall for you;
    It's far too late for my heart.

Unfamiliar (2015)

DESIRE? NEED? LOVE?
    I am not sure
    Which of these
    Has the most power
    In my soul just now.
    All three unfamiliar
    After the eight-year hiatus;
    The complete void of
    All such emotions.
    And you enticed me
    Into your world.
    Where intelligence and sensuality abound
    And they came rushing back.
    There is now a constant
    Ebb and flow of
    Desire. Need. Love.

Unbroken (2015)

WHAT COMPROMISES YOU?
Deep, soulful eyes.
The sexiest mouth ever made.
Strength within and without.
A gigantic, romantic heart—
Scarred and broken—but
Waiting to be healed and whole.
Just like mine.
Intelligence. Wit.
A gentle voice and laugh.
More sex appeal than
Should have been given any man.
There is no hope of
Turning from you now.
Let me show you that
Neither of us is
Too broken to fit together
And love again.

Winter Wishes (2015)

AT THE END OF DECEMBER
    I long for cold nights
    That inspire the use of
    Thick blankets and
    Call to lovers
    To wrap one another in
    A warm embrace.

Souhait d'hiver

A LA FIN DE DÉCEMBRE
>*Je languis pour les nuits froides*
>*Qui inspirent l'utilisation*
>*De couvertures épaisses*
>*Et appellant aux amoureux*
>*D'envelopper eun de l'autre*
>*Dans une étreinte chaleureuse.*

Untitled (2015)

For I simply cannot
Exist in a world
Where I lack the
Affections of such
A man as you...and
You are a phenomenon.

Missing (2016)

HOW IS IT POSSIBLE
    To miss someone so much
    When you just parted
    A few hours ago?

Pour être (2016)

Pour être enveloppé dans
L'etreinte de l'amour que
Vous vous endormez
Est le meilleur sentiment
Au monde.

Inspiration (2016)

YOU ARE MY INSPIRATION
    To be a better person—
    To never stop learning,
    Growing, evolving. And,
    If we are indeed all
    "just floating along
    Accidental-like on a breeze,"
    Then I am ever grateful
    For the breezes that
    Blew me to you

Pensive Moment (2016)

Why do I feel this way? It's crazy—
Unnatural, bizarre, unnerving.
I adore you so much.
I need you always.
My hours with you are precious.

A Cold Spring (2016)

THE FIRST DAY OF SPRING—
    I am freezing
    Without your touch.

Una Primavera fría

EL PRIMER DÍA DE LA primavera-
me estoy congelando
Sin tu toque

Love (2016)

I AM SO VERY IN LOVE with you.
I need you with me, every day,
For the rest of my life.
I need your touch, your embrace, your kisses.
I want skin on skin every night,
Your breath on my cheek
As we sleep.
I love your sparkling blue eyes,
Your smile, your wit, your charm,
Your spirit.
I require your faith and trust
That I will always choose you.
I require your respect,
Your loyalty, and your help
When my spirit falters
And remembers troubles past.
I love you. I love you!
I need you. I want you.
And right now, I miss you.
I am yours always
And all ways.
Say that you are mine...

Une anée du plus grand amour (2016)

EH BIEN, PREQUE.
Tu ais eu tout mon coeur dès le moment où
Nous nous somes recontrés
Et plus nous sommes ensemble, pluse je t'aime
Tu n'ais pas mon coeur; tu es mon coeur
Encore j'ai du mal à te montrer
Tu me remplis
Je suis à mon bien-aimé,
Et mon bien-aimé est à moi
Je n'ai jamais pensé que je trouverais un tel amour
Et je suis si heureux que je l'ai trouvé en tu

Deuxième (2017)

DONC
    Toujours deuxième
    Un simple jouet
    Dans le jeux où
    Je pensais
    Que j'aperçus
    L'amour vrai

If Seeing is Believing (2017)

I WISH THAT I COULD paint my love
    And show it to the world
    So that everyone could see
    How deep, how vas, how strong, how pure
    Is my love for you.

Arguing for the Sake of It (2016)

YOUR ARDOUR MAKES ME amorous

Escape (2016)

WHERE YOU ARE HAS BECOME my solace—refuge—haven.
It is the one place I can escape for a bit.
I hope you understand that.

Vows (2020)

I CHOOSE YOU
    To be no other than yourself,
    Loving all I know of you,
    For you are the one person
    With whom I can share
    All that I am.
    I promise to trust you and be honest with you.
    I promise to listen to you,
    Respect you, and support you.
    I promise to play and laugh with you.
    And grow and bend with you.
    I promise to cherish every day we have together,
    Always and in all ways,
    For you are blood of my blood
    And bone of my bone.
    I take all of you and give you all of me.
    I love you, mo chroí.

About the Author

Miranda Forster grew up in small-town rural Georgia. Her grandparents, parents, siblings, and friends from around the world helped to inspire her writings.

Miranda first fell in love with writing poetry as a young child, and in high school won multiple poetry writing contests.

She says, "Writing is cathartic. It helps me to get out my emotions and be able to come back later and reflect."

Miranda lives in the southern suburbs of Atlanta with her husband, one of two daughters, one cat, and one dog.

She plans to continue to write for the rest of her life.

9 781393 897576